D0646885

SWEDEN

SWEDEN

PHOTOGRAPHY BY CHAD EHLERS

TEXT BY LARS NORDSTRÖM

GRAPHIC ARTS CENTER PUBLISHING COMPANY, PORTLAND, OREGON

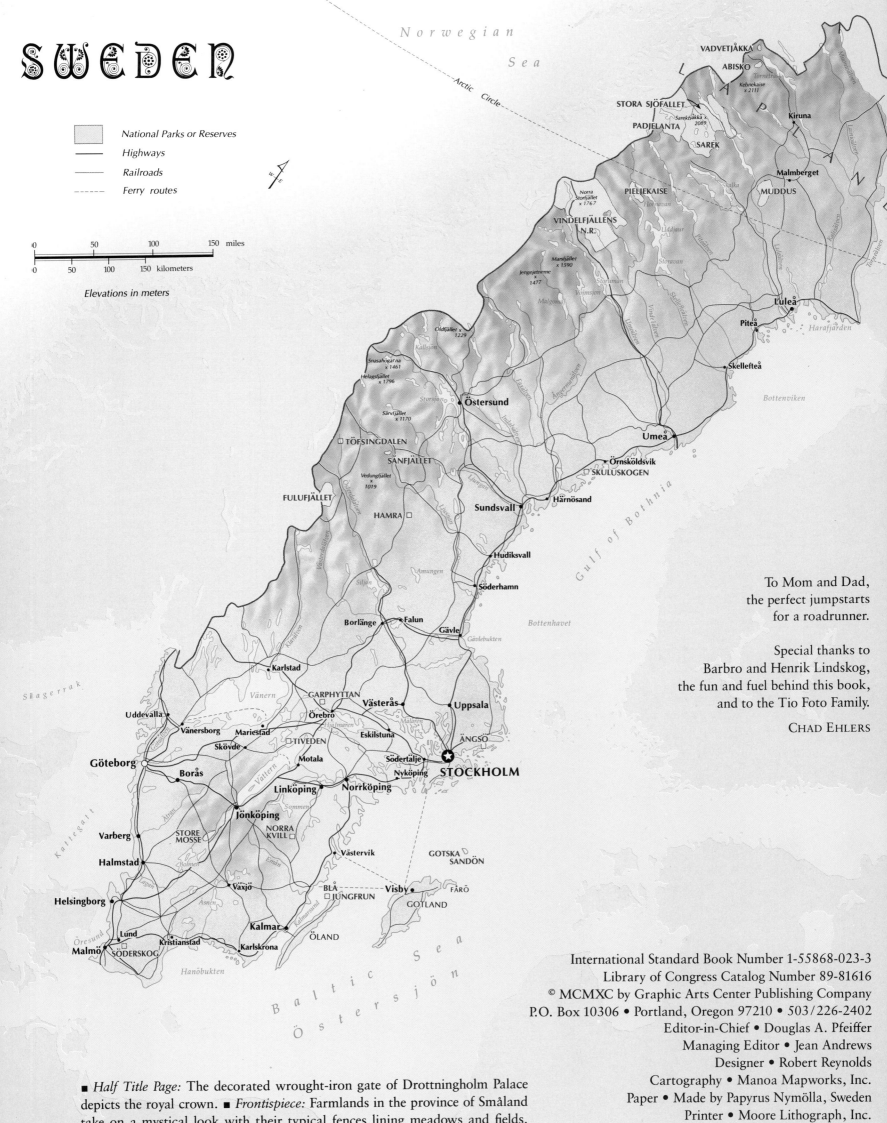

SWEDEN

Legend:
- National Parks or Reserves
- Highways
- Railroads
- Ferry routes

Elevations in meters

Norwegian Sea

Arctic Circle

LAPLAND

VADVETJÅKKA
ABISKO
Kebnekaise x 2111
STORA SJÖFALLET
PADJELANTA
Sarektjåkkå x 2089
SAREK
Kiruna
Malmberget
MUDDUS
PIELJEKAISE
Norra Storfjället x 1767
VINDELFJÄLLENS N.R.
Marsfjället x 1590
Jengejetneme x 1477
Luleå
Piteå
Harafjärden
Oldfjället x 1229
Skellefteå
Snasahögarna x 1461
Helagsfjället x 1796
Östersund
Särvfjället x 1170
Umeå
Örnsköldsvik
SKULESKOGEN
TÖFSINGDALEN
SÄNFJÄLLET
Härnösand
Vedungfjället x 1019
Sundsvall
FULUFJÄLLET
HAMRA
Hudiksvall
Söderhamn
Borlänge Falun
Gävle
Gävlebukten
Karlstad
Vänern
GARPHYTTAN
Västerås
Uppsala
Uddevalla
Örebro
Vänersborg
Mariestad
Eskilstuna
ÄNGSÖ
Skövde
TIVEDEN
Göteborg
Motala
Södertälje
Borås
Linköping
Nyköping
STOCKHOLM
Norrköping
Jönköping
NORRA KVILL
STORE MOSSE
Varberg
Västervik
GOTSKA SANDÖN
Halmstad
Växjö
BLÅ JUNGFRUN
Visby
FÅRÖ
Helsingborg
GOTLAND
Lund
Kalmar
ÖLAND
Kristianstad
Malmö
SÖDERSKOG
Karlskrona
Hanöbukten

Bottenviken
Gulf of Bothnia
Bottenhavet
Baltic Sea / Östersjön
Skagerrak
Kattegatt
Öresund

To Mom and Dad,
the perfect jumpstarts
for a roadrunner.

Special thanks to
Barbro and Henrik Lindskog,
the fun and fuel behind this book,
and to the Tio Foto Family.

CHAD EHLERS

International Standard Book Number 1-55868-023-3
Library of Congress Catalog Number 89-81616
© MCMXC by Graphic Arts Center Publishing Company
P.O. Box 10306 • Portland, Oregon 97210 • 503/226-2402
Editor-in-Chief • Douglas A. Pfeiffer
Managing Editor • Jean Andrews
Designer • Robert Reynolds
Cartography • Manoa Mapworks, Inc.
Paper • Made by Papyrus Nymölla, Sweden
Printer • Moore Lithograph, Inc.
Bindery • Lincoln & Allen
Printed in the United States of America

■ *Half Title Page:* The decorated wrought-iron gate of Drottningholm Palace depicts the royal crown. ■ *Frontispiece:* Farmlands in the province of Småland take on a mystical look with their typical fences lining meadows and fields.

merging out of the Ice Age, Sweden was born ten thousand years ago. Swedes, always enthusiastic about the out-of-doors, see evidence of the Ice Age all the time, and a visitor should not be surprised to hear it casually referred to in conversation. At the beginning of the Ice Age as the ice started to grow, boulders, stones, and small rocks in the bottom of the ice worked as an enormous, rough piece of sandpaper, smoothing everything in the glacier's path. In some places, the grinding power of the ice graded the landscape all the way down to the ancient bedrock. This bedrock, still exposed after ten thousand years, is especially prominent along the coasts where waves, winds, and winter ice have kept it clear of vegetation. In summer, these smooth, clean rocks are appreciated by sun-bathers and swimmers.

The grinding ice also created Sweden's soils, which contain various mixes of large gravel, sand, or very fine clays, depending on the type of rock the ice cap passed over. Because of these moraine deposits, there is little land (10 percent) suitable for crops and pasture. Granite and gneiss are common in Sweden, some as old as 2.7 billion years, making it some of the oldest rock on earth.

Massive stone walls and rock piles along fields in parts of the country, like Småland in the southeast, are evidence that farmers often had backbreaking jobs clearing fields from these intermixed glacial deposits. Other evidence of the polishing power of the ice is the soft, rounded shape of the Swedish mountains in the north.

Far from any geologic faults, neither plate tectonics nor volcanic activities is present to rebuild sharp mountains. The geological stability of the region also means there are no earthquakes. One drawback, of course, is that there are no hot springs to be found either. But because the Finns have taught the Swedes the pleasures of saunas instead, that form of recreation has become an important way of enduring the long, cold Swedish winters.

Grinding glacial ice also created countless hollows and basins which became lakes. Of Sweden's total surface area today, more than 15 percent is covered by water. There are some thirty major rivers and about ninety thousand lakes, including Lake Vänern, Western Europe's largest fresh-water lake. It covers 5,546 square kilometers (2,141 square miles), an area slightly larger than Delaware.

■ *Preceding Page:* The Hälsinge-Hambo folk dance festival includes dancing, national and local costumes, and musicians. Folk dancing—with picnicking, more folk dancing, and even a siesta—is routine at the competition. ■ *Right:* The arteries of the country are its rivers. The Rapadalen with its river delta is a great place for water and hiker to meander their way through a land of line, space, and color within endless vistas of snow-capped, undulating mountain ranges.

T hat Swedish river valleys are characteristically U-shaped rather than V-shaped is also explained by the Ice Age forces; their shapes do not result from erosion caused by the rivers eating their way down as is common in other regions, but from the water that moved evenly under the ice.

Then there is the almost ubiquitous presence of the huge boulders that are scattered throughout the landscape, giving Swedish woods and farmlands their special feeling. These boulders were carried inside the glacier, then dropped as the ice melted. In the old days, many villages established one of these rocks as a "lifting rock," where the young men of the community would try their strength. More than one moss-covered boulder also had a firm place in the local legends of battles between giants who threw the massive stones at each other, and the impressive size, shape, and color of these boulders have inspired artists for many centuries. Boulders with identifying features such as cracks or trees growing on them, especially along roads or major waterways, still get special names and become well-known reference points.

What is perhaps more astonishing is that the Ice Age is still actively shaping the landscape. Scientists estimate that the ice cap was about two miles thick at its mightiest, and two miles of ice translates into a lot of weight at the bottom. Because the glacial ice remained in place for thousands of years, it pressed the land down into the soft, molten core of the earth.

When the ice retreated, the land began to spring back, a process that is still continuing today. How long this process will go on, no one really knows, but Sweden will probably continue to "grow" out of the sea, and its landscape will continue to be transformed. Shallow bays in the Baltic will gradually become meadows or forests. Uppsala, an old city approximately seventy kilometers (forty-five miles) north of Stockholm, was accessible by ocean-going Viking ships a thousand years ago. It is now well inland, surrounded by great, flat, farmed fields. Only creeks and small, slowly moving rivers still remain today of the once-brackish inlets and waterways, and it takes more than an hour to travel from Uppsala to the Baltic Coast by car.

> ■ *Left:* The encounter between land and sea is a timeless story of constant jousting between forces of creation and those of destruction. On the west coast, everything is on a large scale, lines are broad, and the sea breathes deeply. The east coast, with its multitude of larger and smaller islands, quieter winds, and more subdued seas, evokes memories of a freshwater landscape.

he retreat of the ice also marked the start of Sweden's animal and plant life. Since so much water was still trapped in the ice cap before all the ice had melted, ocean levels were considerably lower than today, and it is believed there was a land bridge between Denmark and Sweden. Across this bridge, all plants, insects, birds, animals, and other living things that had been pushed south to the European continent during the expansion of the ice now moved back. The sparse vegetation in the northern mountains today probably resembles what the edge of the advancing vegetation looked like at that time. For example, oaks still have not spread north of the Dalälven River, which is only a third of the way up into the country, and small oak and beech forests are only to be found in the southern part of Sweden. A few animals, such as the European bison, were eventually pushed to extinction before modern times. Others like the wild boar, have been successfully reintroduced; and a few new exotic species, such as the Greenland musk ox, have been brought in by man.

Sweden is the fourth-largest country in Europe, covering nearly 500,000 square kilometers (200,000 square miles). Established in 1751 and following a natural mountain ridge, the border between Sweden and Norway stretches 1,619 kilometers (1,000 miles). On the Swedish side, rivers run eastward toward the Gulf of Bothnia; on the Norwegian side, westward toward the Atlantic. Sweden is part of a peninsula, so its coastline is long, about 2,500 kilometers (1,500 miles). The country is divided into three main regions—Norrland, meaning "northern lands," Svealand, and Götaland—and twenty-five provinces. The two southern regions are named for tribes that once lived in these regions, the *Svear,* Swedes, and the *Götar,* Goths. Off the southeastern coast are two islands, Öland and Gotland.

The major farming areas are in southern Sweden, south of Lake Vänern, and in central Sweden around Lake Mälaren. In northern Sweden, the growing season is too short for wheat. In Svealand and Götaland, the farmed areas are dotted with lakes, woodlands, and small forests; but in Norrland, the forests clearly dominate the landscape. Norrland is also where the mountains start. Mount Kebnekaise is the highest at 2,111 meters (almost 7,000 feet). Areas of open highland stretch across ridge after ridge of mountain terrain.

■ *Right:* Nature's architecture in winter, such as here on Åreskutan above Åre, carries a little harder jurisdiction. The sounds of spring, summer, and autumn are not heard as often as the frozen vŏice of winter. Things—including ears, noses, fingers, and cameras—start to get brittle at these temperatures.

As the traditional summer territory of the Laplanders, or *Saamis*, and haven for cross-country skiers and hikers, this is an area of magnificent views and a sense of eternity. National parks here are called "Europe's last wilderness." Elsewhere, trails are clearly marked and dotted at intervals by cabins with beds and cooking facilities.

Sweden is approximately the same size as California, but longer and narrower. Superimposed over North America, all of Sweden would be north of the continental United States. The southern tip would be in British Columbia, with the country extending north to the oil drilling rigs on Alaska's North Slope. Due to the relatively warm waters brought to northwestern Europe by the Gulf Stream, the climate of Sweden is much milder than that of Alaska or the Canadian interior. In winter, southern and southwestern Sweden resembles much more the Pacific Northwest, mostly rain with some snow. However, in Sweden's capital, Stockholm, annual precipitation averages only 560 millimeters per year—a mere 22 inches. The Oregon coast may get that much in one rainy winter month. Winters in most of Sweden are usually white. Every February, when the schools get a week of "sporting vacation," innumerable families strap skis and poles to the roof rack, crowd into their cars with a week's worth of food and clothing, and head off to a cabin in the mountains. In late winter or early spring, fishing on the ice is very popular.

Spring arrives in mid-March in the south, mid- to late April in central Sweden, and late May in the north. In contrast to Pacific Northwest springs, Swedish springs are usually a furious battle between winter and spring, with cold hanging on in spite of lengthening daylight. Then spring triumphs, and in two weeks it might be all over, the forest changed from bare to leafy. *Valborgsmässoafton*, a pre-Christian holiday celebrating the death of winter and arrival of spring, is on the last day of April. That evening, large bonfires are lit, spring songs are sung, speeches are given, and poems are read.

The most remarkable thing about summer in Sweden is probably the light, and for that reason June is the year's most magical month. The mosquitoes hum incessantly, and flowers and birdsong are everywhere. The air is filled with smells, and for all those who have endured the Swedish winter, this is a time for rejoicing.

■ *Left:* A common early morning sight across the whole of a country with cold nights, wet meadows, and over ninety thousand lakes, here a small lake and its surrounding area in Småland are covered with a thin fog, a single silence sleeping over land and water. The mist slides across meadow, lake, and forest floor until the sun chases it away, leaving a slight steam to curl along the surface.

It is no wonder that ancient pagan celebrations at summer solstice have survived completely intact after a thousand years of Christianity. People still decorate the maypole, put flower wreaths on their heads, dance, eat, and drink until the sun returns in the early morning hours. According to tradition, a girl may pick seven different kinds of flowers on Midsummer Night's Eve. She must pick in silence and remain silent until she has put them under her pillow. If everything is done properly, she then may dream of her future husband.

In some parts of the country, such as Dalarna, midsummer is a time to see folk costumes, hear fiddle music, and watch the traditional folk dances. Midsummer is also a time when school is out and no one can tell anyone to go to bed. Even children stay up as late as they like.

The forest has always been integrated into Swedish life, providing building material, pulp, firewood, charcoal, tar, wild game, berries, mushrooms, and recreation. About half of Sweden's area is forest, mostly pine, spruce, and birch, though many more varieties appear to the discerning eye. Today, forest areas are actually increasing because many small, abandoned farms are being replanted into forest. Compared to the rest of Europe, Sweden has the largest reserve of soft woods, and it is the world's sixth-largest timber producer. Because northern trees take 90 to 150 years to mature, Sweden's forests are carefully managed with an annual cut 15 percent below growth.

But just as farms have developed into large units, so have wood lots. It has been so difficult for ordinary citizens to get permission from government agencies to acquire small woodlots that a fairly heated political discussion has surfaced about the policy's democratic justification. Clear-cutting practices are also hotly debated, especially in the ecologically sensitive areas below timberline in the northern mountains. According to critics, euphemisms such as "rejuvenation area" instead of "clear cut" are only attempts to hide an ugly reality.

But forest lands are not only valuable for timber, they are also an important source of berries and mushrooms. First are wild raspberries and strawberries in July, followed by blueberries. Later, the northern cloudberry, often called "marsh gold," ripens. In years when cloudberries are scarce, hostilities have developed between locals and pickers from other areas. In September, it is time for lingonberries.

■ *Right:* Along the northeast coast, on the tip of a long spit surrounded by water, stands the Högby Lighthouse. A small quiet bay on one side and the more restless Baltic Sea on the other, this picturesque setting is a fitting residence for the painter Stephan Lundh and his Ancient Mariner-like studio. The bay, the studio and the lighthouse seem to create the perfect surroundings for the artist.

If you ask a Swede where he picks berries, you will get a mysterious smile and the vaguest of directions, if any at all. Instead, he will most likely tell you an anecdote about something that happened once when he was picking berries. A good berry place is a family secret.

In recent years, the money in commercial berry picking in the woods has been enough to attract students from eastern Europe, especially Poland. In a good berry year, two months of hard work can pay for a year at the university in Poland.

Except for the spring morels, mushroom season starts in mid-July if the weather has been wet enough. Most pickers harvest chanterelles and boletus mushrooms, but many pick other varieties as well. Mushroom places, like berry places, are well-guarded secrets.

Hunting continues to be important. Several factors have influenced the growth of animal populations like moose. These factors include an altered forest ecology due to clear-cutting, more ecologically educated hunters who spare reproductive animals, and a dwindling number of domestic animals grazing in the woods. In the mid-1850s, about a thousand moose were killed annually; today, these figures are 150 to 200 thousand. Guns are controlled, as are hunting rights. To buy a gun, one must prove the right to use it; that comes with owning forest property or buying, leasing, or inheriting hunting rights.

For most people who live in highly urbanized areas, time spent in the woods is especially relished. All woods activities are possible because of a unique right called *allemansrätten,* meaning "every man's right." This is the right to walk freely everywhere except close to a private home or, of course, on farmed fields. Otherwise, anyone can hike and pick berries and mushrooms in the woods. If one is far from private houses, camping is also permitted so long as living plants are not harmed. Weather permitting, one may even start a fire.

Swedish family names—if not Andersson, Johansson, Svensson, or some other "son of somebody"—likely come from nature. My own family name, *Nordström,* means "Northern Stream." And there are names like "Branch of the Linden Tree," *Lindgren;* "Flower," *Blom;* "Stony Ground," *Stenmark;* or "Mountain Man," *Bergman.* Even first names, like "Rock," *Sten,* or "Wolf," *Ulf,* are from nature. And who would play tennis with a man called "Bear Castle," *Björn Borg?*

■ *Left:* Much of the landscape is dominated by coniferous forests, which in southern Sweden blend with deciduous woods and forests. Deciduous trees in varying raiments are a living symbol of the four seasons. This beech forest is one of the few in Skåne on the southwestern coast not replaced by farms.

**A**lthough no more than sixty thousand Laplanders, who call themselves *Saamis*, are spread over four nations, they are surprisingly well known worldwide. Their nomadic way of life—centered around reindeer, hunting, and fishing in a harsh but stunningly beautiful part of the world—stirs something deep within. With them, we share what all shared before the arrival of agriculture, cities, or governments. But in our rapidly changing technological society, the life of these people is changing as well.

Forty thousand Saamis live in northern Norway, about fifteen thousand in Sweden, four thousand in Finland, and fifteen hundred to two thousand in the USSR. Their area, called Lapland by the English-speaking world but *Saamiätnam* by the Saamis themselves, stretches from the southern point of the mountains across northern Sweden and Norway, Finland north of the Arctic Circle, and most of the Kola Peninsula in the USSR. Encompassing about 150 thousand square miles, this area is almost as large as Sweden itself.

The word Lappland is used in Sweden, but there it only designates the northernmost province of the country. Many Swedish Saamis live outside Lappland. Though the term *Saami* is now the one used by most people as well as by radio, television, and newspapers, the term *Lapp* is more or less restricted to legal and government language.

The Saamis have lived in Saamiätnam since time immemorial. No one really knows where they came from. The most widely held theory derives its evidence from the relationships of languages in the Finno-Ugric language group and anthropological studies of related peoples in the north. This theory holds that the Saamis must have originated somewhere in Russia, north of where Moscow is today. At the end of the Ice Age, they followed the reindeer north, some moving through Finland into northern Scandinavia and down through its mountains, some moving directly north onto the Kola Peninsula. The Finns, with similar origins but different customs, came later.

Clearly, the Saami language is closely related to Finnish, but it differs enough that Finns and Saamis cannot speak with each other. Because Saamis have lived over such a vast area for so long, their language has developed into separate dialects. When Saamis from the south meet with those from the north, they often speak Swedish.

Saamis

> ■ *Right:* All of Härjedalen Province is the highest in Sweden, with no point less than a thousand feet above sea level. These smooth plateaus and imposing peaks near Ljungdalen offer good skiing and mountaineering. The mountains and mires mix with tranquility and silence to make this a haven of unspoiled scenery.

owever, when they work with the reindeer, they always use their own language because only it contains the necessary terminology. What is truly remarkable about the Saami language is that approximately one-quarter of the vocabulary refers to reindeer. Though only twenty-five hundred of the fifteen thousand Saamis in Sweden are involved in reindeer herding, it is they who capture the imagination.

During the last fifty years, the Saamis have organized themselves across the national boundaries separating them, thus strengthening their ethnic identity. They now learn their native tongue in school, and books in Saami are available in increasing numbers. Some radio stations even have regular Saami broadcasts, and in Sweden there is at least one major Saami magazine. The study of Saami culture has finally been established at a Swedish university as well. Saami literary culture has also flowered in recent years with poems, short stories, fiction, and memoirs published in Saami, Swedish, and Norwegian.

Reindeer herding, the essence of traditional Saami life, has evolved into a large-scale business. But keeping semidomesticated reindeer has been part of Saami culture for a long time. Females were kept for milking, and though a reindeer does not yield more than half a cup per day, the milk is very rich. With a 17 percent fat content, reindeer milk is made into cheese which is used in coffee.

Castrated male reindeer were tamed and used for different tasks. In winter, they were hitched to small, boat-shaped sleighs, which were built like boats with sterns, keels, bulwarks, and ribs (no runners). More like boats than sleighs, there is no English word for them. There were many different kinds of these sleighs — some were used to carry food and goods; others, people. Scandinavian Saamis utilized only one reindeer to pull each sleigh. The Saamis on the Kola Peninsula, on the other hand, hitched a team of males to a larger sleigh. (Santa Claus may be a Kola Peninsula Saami in disguise!)

Reindeer migrate in an annual cycle from low-elevation forest land in winter to high-elevation open mountain range in summer. During the entire year, Saamis follow and attend the reindeer. In the old days, they spent the winter in a *goathi,* a permanent, conical hut made of poles covered with birch bark and peat moss. During the migrations, they lived in movable structures similar to the American Indian tepee.

■ *Left:* Calf-marking is often a family project. This round-up in normal dress is more in line with present reality than are photos of Lapps, or *Saamis,* in colorful costumes smiling for tourist cameras. They no longer live in huts or traditional dress. The brightly colored Saami costume is more a holiday dress, and the huts are mostly for tourists to use as exotic backdrops for their pictures. Some huts are still used when the Saami are out collecting fish, fowl, or reindeer.

Today, reindeer-herding Saamis spend winters in modern houses, leaving a few herders with snowmobiles to keep track of the animals and accompany them to spring pastures. During summer, the animals are often watched by helicopter. They are herded collectively by a group of families or "village," but they are individually owned. At summer's end, they are rounded up and brought down to the calving grounds, where animals from the different villages are separated. Herds of six to eight thousand are not uncommon.

Reindeer once provided most of the Saamis' survival needs; nothing was wasted. Most of the animal is still utilized, and reindeer skins, light and warmer than any other skin, are still popular with hikers as a cozy sleeping pad. New products—such as horns ground up for aphrodisiacs in Japan—are still developing today.

From the Saamis' point of view, the last thousand years represent a decrease in control over their land; from the Kingdom of Sweden's point of view, development of Swedish Saamiätnam represents an increase in access to great natural resources. It was not until the 1600s that development of northern Sweden really started, and then only because the government gave settlers in the north a certain number of tax-free years. With this incentive, farmed areas kept increasing northward along the Gulf of Bothnia and west toward the mountains. But as people moved into this territory, they settled in traditional Saami regions, and conflicts arose. This led to the establishment of the "farming line," a line running north to south, following the contours of the land and separating the reindeer's winter and summer pastures. Farming was not encouraged west of this line.

The other conflict between farmers and Saamis concerned fishing and hunting rights, once reserved entirely for Saamis. Though Saamis were the original inhabitants of the mountains and northern forests, they do not own this land. The state reserves the right to utilize any area if such use is deemed beneficial to the country as a whole.

Besides logging, dams, and tourism, perhaps the greatest blow to reindeer herding was the Chernobyl nuclear disaster in 1986. Radioactive isotopes, absorbed by the lichen that reindeer eat, rendered the meat unfit for human consumption. Though villagers are reimbursed for unsalable meat, the uncertain future worries the Saamis.

> ■ *Right:* Kebnekaise is Sweden's highest peak, rising out of the Scandinavian mountain chain in northwest Lappland. Its two highest points are the South Peak at 2,111 meters (6,925 feet) with its small glacier, and the North Peak at 2,097 meters (6,879 feet) with its adjoining massif and numerous glaciers.

ust as the history of the Saamis goes far back in time to an immigration from the east, the history of the Swedes goes back to an immigration from the south. Sweden's historical clock began ticking as the early Stone Age hunters and gatherers moved onto the Scandinavian Peninsula from the south, following the retreat of the Ice Age glaciers. These people did not farm at all, but lived off the country, moving from place to place according to the season. During the later Stone Age, around 2000 B.C., a wave of new people came to Sweden. They were more stationary than their predecessors, employing axes and basic farming techniques and keeping domesticated animals. These people were Germanic and are most likely the direct ancestors of today's Swedes. In Europe, Sweden is unique in that no other people have had the desire to invade this territory and claim it in a way that displaced the original population.

Change accelerated in the Bronze Age. Agricultural techniques improved, and recent settlers left more traces. On bedrock polished by the Ice Age glacier, they carved petroglyphs depicting suns, boats, human figures, tools, weapons, animals, and other things. One such place, the best known in Sweden, is Tanumshede on the west coast.

During this period and through the Iron Age, unique graves were dug with large stones set in the shape of long ships. During the early part of this period, the province of Västergötland, just north of these petroglyphs and graves, was cleared and settled, making it one of the oldest permanently inhabited areas in Sweden.

The Iron Age, spanning 500 B.C. to 400 A.D., is characterized by a growing ability to manufacture tools, weapons, and necessary hardware. The iron was a local product. It was not mined, but, in winter, people cut holes in the ice and scooped iron ore nodules from the bottom of the lakes. The ore was then heated in small kilns to yield its iron.

With the collapse of the Roman Empire in about 400 A.D., the Folk Migrations began. Many northern European tribes started looking for new places to settle, and Germanic people poured into England. *Beowulf,* a literary work usually considered first in the English tradition, uses western Sweden for much of its setting and western Swedes for many of its characters.

■ *Left:* The archipelago starting in Stockholm some fifty kilometers (thirty miles) and several thousand islands to the west ends here in the Baltic as small, polished, wind-blown skerries. Flowers and fowl are prolific and enjoy little disturbance, as do those sailors who read navigation charts well enough and have adventure enough in their blood to get to these skerries at Lilla Nassa.

In 793, a group of Viking ships raided the unprotected village and monastery of Lindisfarne on England's east coast in a way which was to become typical for the next hundred years. Without warning, several Viking ships pulled up on the beach, landed soldiers, killed the inhabitants, and looted whatever they could lay their hands on. After the ships were loaded with treasures, all the buildings were set on fire and the boats took off.

This event opened the period of the Viking Age, 800 to 1000 A.D. Stories and descriptions left by people who encountered Vikings, from monks in England to Arabic traders in Constantinople, as well as stories Vikings told about themselves in the Icelandic sagas, give us valuable insight. The Vikings left a heritage exhibiting their eminent skills as boat builders, sailors, fearless and cunning warriors, blacksmiths, wood carvers, adventurous traders, undaunted explorers and settlers, and as eloquent poets and story-tellers. Less attention has been given to the other side of Viking life: the slaves they kept, the maiming they used as punishment, or the treachery they often demonstrated toward each other.

Three factors made events of the Viking Age possible. First, it was a warm period, resulting in good harvests and an abundance of food. Consequently, people were healthier, and more children reached adulthood. Second, the inheritance laws of these Scandinavian tribes gave everything to the oldest son: the farm, animals, thralls (or slaves), and boats. If there were younger sons, they had two alternatives: marry into wealth, or go raiding. Finally, the Vikings were able to extend their raids due to superior ships. Their ships had been perfected over centuries in Scandinavia, where water played such a central role in transportation. They were the fastest ships at the time, with a shallow draft making them excellent for rapid beaching. Their design also made them suitable for rivers, where the ships often had to be hauled past waterfalls, or even between different watersheds.

Even if today's most common image of the Viking is the warrior, he was also a settler and trader. The rulers of areas hit by Viking raiders rapidly learned that the best way to avoid future attacks was by granting them power and land. This led to more Scandinavians settling in the areas controlled by Viking chieftains.

■ *Right:* Skåne, sometimes called the "princely province," is densely populated, with excellent estates and more than 240 fascinating castles. One of these higher rent residences is Trolleholm, which is a magnificent castle in the Renaissance style. This castle is unique with pointed towers and staircase gables.

The Vikings were able to communicate with the Germanic tribes that had settled England during the Folk Migrations. There was a commonality in the dialects, traces of which remain today between Swedish and English. A knife is called a *kniv,* but Swedish pronounces both the "k" and the "n." On a ship, the right side is called "starboard," *(styrbord* in Swedish), because Viking ships had their rudder, or "steering board," on the ship's right side. "Window" has its origin in the Viking dwelling, the smoke hole called the "wind's eye."

Most of the Swedish Vikings went eastward, across the Baltic into what is now the Soviet Union, to trade and loot. In this part of the world they were known as "Rhos" or "Rus," and it is believed that the dynasty of "Rus" kings established at Kiev in the early 900s gave Russia its name. Historical records document that Swedish Vikings, whether soldiers or traders, always traveled fully armed with sword, axe, and knife. Few of those who left ever made it back with any riches. There are many rune stones in Sweden that commemorate a husband or brother who, as it was often expressed at the time, "fed the eagles," or died. The last great Viking expedition eastward from Sweden set forth in 1041, marking the end of the Viking period.

The rule of King Olof Skötkonung opened the Middle Ages. He had adopted the Christian faith in 1008 and united the Swedes and the Goths into one kingdom. Birka, the old center of commerce, had played out its role, and the capital was established in Sigtuna, a town to the north. Still on the shores of Lake Mälaren, it was located about forty kilometers south of Uppsala, which remained a heathen city for another hundred years. The first Swedish coins were minted in Sigtuna, which became a center for Anglo-Saxon missionary activity. Still, Sweden was far from being a powerful and secure nation. As late as 1187, a small army of descendants of the Vikings who had settled on the east coast of the Baltic sailed into Sigtuna, looted the town, and destroyed it.

The church, through its clergy, land holdings, monasteries, and tax-free status, rapidly gained influence and became prominent politically. With the Pope's blessing to spread Christianity, the conquest of Finland commenced in 1157, beginning a long Swedish rule over Finland, which served as a buffer against the Russians.

> ■ *Left:* The fiery red "vallmo" flower can flood or sprinkle itself across the farmlands of spring and summer. Despite a sharp reduction in the number of farms and crop acreage, production has increased more than demand in Sweden. This farm is near Hässleholm in Skåne and is typical of this rolling province.

ociety was still dominated by social structures inherited from the Vikings, with the family or clan as the central cohesive force. Separation between free men and slaves was maintained until the 1330s.

Sweden's oldest preserved written documents date from the thirteenth century, when, for the first time, laws regulating ownership and inheritance were written down. Stockholm, strategically located where Lake Mälaren drains into the salt waters of the Baltic, was founded around 1250. Due to increased metal production in central Sweden, the economy grew, and trade was developed through the German Hanseatic League in the Baltic. This was also the period in which the aristocracy developed and, with the clergy, gained political influence with the king. Around 1350, the entire Swedish kingdom was unified under one law, though the borders kept changing because of political instability.

The later Middle Ages were marked by endless battles between Swedes and Danes over who was to gain dominance. In 1389, Danish Queen Margarete managed to unify Denmark, Norway, and Sweden, but the Swedes rebelled and broke free from the union, viewing it as an occupation. Though the Scandinavian countries have remained close, unification has never been accomplished again.

The Middle Ages came to an end when Gustav Vasa finally drove the Danes out of central Sweden in 1521. Crowned king in 1523, Vasa made Stockholm the capital of Sweden. Surely no metropolis at the time, Stockholm had approximately three hundred taxpayers and an estimated population of five thousand. In 1527, as a result of the Reformation, Sweden broke with the Catholic church, and practically all of the church's holdings became the property either of the state or the aristocracy. Power was centralized around the king, and a substantial government organization slowly emerged. In 1526, the New Testament was published in Swedish, and in 1541, the entire Bible, helping to create modern Swedish. Vasa is credited with the well-known saying, "Everyone wants the axe to move but nobody wants to hold the handle," but it is clear from his reign that he did not really mind holding the handle himself. Just before his death, King Vasa set up a hereditary kingdom in Sweden, a system still in existence today.

■ *Right:* Öland is known as the island of windmills, which add to the beautiful character of this long level limestone plateau. Numerous windmills can be seen scattered across the island, or in rows along the tors. Many are in the last stage of disrepair, while some have been converted into living quarters.

In the seventeenth century, Sweden emerged as one of Europe's leading powers. Not only were there large territories around the Baltic in Swedish hands during this time, but Sweden moved beyond the limits of Europe. In 1638, Fort Christina, named after the Swedish Queen Christina, was established in the New World. This colony in North America was located at the mouth of the Delaware River, where Wilmington is today. It was short-lived and soon lost to the Dutch, another emerging European naval power, but historians often credit it with contributing to the settling of the American wilderness something absolutely essential: the log cabin. This basic building technique, practiced all over Sweden, Norway, and Finland at the time, provided the American settler with a method of converting trees into houses with nothing more than an axe.

The eighteenth century was marked by modern impulses shared by the rest of Europe and the United States. New ideas of freedom and political reform were born. New discoveries in science and biology led to new views of the world. Active trade with distant countries in the Far East brought new goods and ideas to European culture. In the early part of the century, the power of the king was temporarily diminished and replaced by the power of the parliament, made up of representatives of the four estates: the aristocracy, the clergy, the merchants, and the farmers. For the first time, political parties emerged as important forces. There was political support for manufacturing, and a new element of the economy started to grow.

In 1735, Swedish botanist Linnaeus published *Systema Naturae*, which sowed the seeds for the science of biological taxonomy by establishing the foundation for naming and classifying plant and animal species. Around the same time, Swedish astronomer Anders Celsius devised a thermometer where the range between freezing and boiling water (0 and 100) was divided into one hundred parts, which are commonly called centigrades. In 1767, the Swedish population reached two million. In 1786, the Swedish Academy was founded to study and protect the language by creating a dictionary to standardize proper spelling and pronunciation. Today, the academy is perhaps best known for its annual choice of a Nobel laureate of literature — and it still publishes a dictionary.

■ *Left:* Sandhamn, in Stockholm's outer archipelago, has two of the finest yacht racing courses in the world. Over five hundred sailing boats compete in a variety of classes in the race around Gotland, or Gotland Runt. Depending on the winds, the race takes about three days to circle the island and return to Sandhamn.

Sweden Now

During the early nineteenth century, Sweden was drawn into the turmoil of Napoleonic Europe, forming a coalition with England against France. Russia attacked Swedish Finland in 1807, and in 1809, after six hundred years of Swedish rule, Finland was lost to Russia. As a result, a reform of the political system took place in 1809, based on the principles of shared political power, and further restricting the power of the king. In 1814, in the last war Sweden has ever fought, Sweden participated in a campaign against Napoleon.

The nineteenth century saw the continuation and acceleration of various reforms and reorganizations that had begun earlier. The liberal opposition demanded an end to an independent royal rule and to the parliament of the four estates. Around the middle of the century, railroads were built, factories were erected, and large-scale logging of northern Sweden was begun. More and more people moved to the cities. The situation of women showed improvement, the penitentiary system was humanized, and again there was an increase in religious freedom. Toward the end of the century, Sweden was seriously drawn into the industrial revolution.

Around 1850, the emigration to the United States began in earnest. The primary motivation was poverty, but there were also numerous emigrants who left because they felt they lacked religious freedom under the Swedish Lutheran state church. Many early colonists in the 1850s followed various religious leaders and ended up in utopian communes in the United States. The well-known, but brief, Erik Jansar colony at Bishop Hill, Illinois, claimed to have seven hundred members in 1853 and owned sixty-four hundred acres of land.

Swedish emigration increased dramatically during the famine years of 1867 and 1868. Due to unusually cold summers, crops failed, and large numbers of people faced the choice of starvation or emigration. The provinces hardest hit by the poor harvests and mass emigration were Småland, Västergötland, Värmland, and most of the Norrland region. In Norrland, entire villages emigrated, leaving the forest to reclaim their small patches of cleared land. Large, poor populations from the major cities also left for a new life in the New World. The first wave of immigrants came via New York and Chicago and settled mainly in the Midwest, in Minnesota or on the western prairies.

■ *Right:* The emphasis in Swedish sports is not on competition between schools, but is more between clubs, organizations, and on a personal level. One of the major events is the Vansbro Swim, *Vansbrosimningen,* in July at Vansbro in Dalarna. This is a swim of three kilometers (nearly two miles) downstream in the river Vanån and one kilometer (two-thirds mile) upstream in Västerdals River. About nineteen hundred participants start, including 250 competitors.

hen, as the Pacific Northwest became accessible by train in the 1880s, a second wave of immigrants continued west. Estimates are that from 1850 to 1920, 15 to 20 percent of the entire Swedish population immigrated to the United States. Put another way, by 1910, every fifth Swede lived in North America. Most of the early immigrants found new lives as farmers or loggers, though populations of Swedes later developed in cities like Chicago, Minneapolis, and Seattle.

Unfortunately, the language and culture of the Swedes in America disappeared quickly. The immigrants spoke Swedish as their first language, and their children understood it. But they were unable to speak the language fluently and transmit it to their children. The third generation usually retained just a handful of words as their entire heritage of the Swedish language. A small Swedish press grew, flourished, and died in less than a hundred years. Today, there are no daily Swedish newspapers, though a few weekly newsletters persist. Literary critics claim Swedish literature and writing in the United States became a closed chapter before World War II.

Swedish cultural expressions met the same fate as the language; Swedish-Americans considered visiting Swedes "foreigners," implying their American identity was primary. Just as few words of Swedish have survived in third- and fourth-generation "Swedes," only a handful of symbolic cultural expressions like Swedish gingersnaps or folk dancing remain. To paraphrase the American poet Robert Frost, culture is what gets lost in emigration.

During the last hundred years, Sweden has emerged as one of the world's wealthiest and most industrial nations. As in most highly industrialized societies, this change has also meant a continuous flow of people from the country to the cities. Once a nation of poor, rural residents, today more than 80 percent of Sweden's population lives in cities. In 1850, Stockholm numbered one hundred thousand people of a total population of four million. Today, Stockholm has 1.5 million; the country as a whole, 8.5 million. The metropolitan areas around Stockholm, Göteborg, and Malmö account for almost a third of the entire urban population. The northern two-thirds of the country, with only 10 percent of the population, still sends a steady trickle of young people southward.

■ *Left:* With its seventy-six-hundred-kilometer (forty-six-hundred-mile) coastline, surrounded by nearly nontidal seas and serrated by innumerable bays and inlets, and with its fantastic archipelago with intricate networks of sounds and literally thousands of islands and skerries, Sweden becomes a yachting paradise.

wo factors that have contributed to Sweden's development are the emigration to North America, which eased the domestic demand for both land and jobs, and the European demand for Swedish wood products and iron during the second half of the nineteenth century. Since industrialization occurred earlier in England and Germany than it did in Sweden, Europe needed the natural resources that were available from Sweden.

Necessity is the mother of invention, and as industries were established in Sweden, a series of important Swedish inventions between 1855 and 1923 contributed to the success of the emerging industrial nation: the safety match, dynamite, the milk and cream separator, the zipper, the primus stove, the adjustable crescent wrench, the self-aligning ball bearing, the mechanism that turns lighthouse lights on and off, improvements on the telephone, the taximeter, the condensation mechanism for refrigerators, and the fan-operated vacuum cleaner. Many of these inventions were the founding basis for several Swedish companies still in operation around the world today and belong to Sweden's industrial base. There were other consequences, too. For example, the Nobel prizes, created by Alfred Nobel, the inventor of dynamite, focus world attention on Sweden as the awards are handed out in Stockholm each December. The Nobel prizes have, perhaps more than anything else, contributed to the nation's international reputation.

The modern Swedish political system was also formed as the nation became more industrialized. It can be described as a constitutional monarchy and parliamentary democracy, with constitutional power divided between the ruling party government and the parliament. Following a constitutional reform in the early 1970s, the role of the king became purely symbolic and representative. The king opens the new parliament every year and represents Sweden at many international events, but he lacks any real political power. In 1976, the present king, Carl XVI Gustav, married a German commoner, Silvia Sommerlath. Their first-born child, Princess Victoria, now stands in line to be Sweden's next royal regent. When she inherits the throne from her father, she will become Sweden's first queen since Queen Christina held the throne.

■ *Right:* At night the *Avenyen,* the avenue leading to Götaplatsen, with its imposing floodlit gallery and the fountain group by Carl Milles, is bustling with life. People from Gothenburg will tell you there is more contact between people in this city than is experienced by those living in the capital of Stockholm.

he constitutional reform in the early 1970s also changed the two-chamber parliament of 1866 into a one-chamber parliament with 349 seats. Of those seats, 310 are elected directly, and the remaining 39 are appointed in proportion to the distribution of votes among the political parties. There is a 4-percent threshold to get into parliament, which means that unless a party receives at least 4 percent of the vote, it will not be represented.

Five of the six major political parties can trace their origins to the turn of the century, and trade unions that emerged then are still a powerful force. Swedish elections, carried out every three years with almost 90 percent of the population voting, traditionally concern political programs put forth by parties rather than by individuals. Each party member agrees to represent the party platform, and the citizens vote for the program of their choice. Women hold thirty percent of the parliamentary seats.

The five largest political parties range from socialist to conservative, with two choosing a liberal middle ground. A new sixth one, an environmental party, was recently voted into parliament. It adopts both socialist and conservative elements, although political observers see it as primarily liberal. Since trade unions, which are closely allied with Social Democrats, remain a powerful force in Swedish politics, it is not surprising that Social Democrats have been the clearly dominant political force in Sweden. With the exception of two liberal-conservative coalitions from 1976 to 1982, the Social Democrats have ruled Sweden continuously since World War II.

Much of what the world finds interesting about the Swedish system can be traced back to the policies of social equality and democracy shaped by the Social Democrats. Even the term, "ombudsman," one of the few modern Swedish words to have made its way into the English language, comes from the political reality of the post-war period. Many claim the state suffers from a "big brother syndrome," meaning it assumes responsibilities which are none of its business. A typical example in this debate is Sweden's strict alcohol policy. Alcohol (everything except light beer) is restricted to a government monopoly. Sold through special stores open only forty-five hours per week to people over twenty years of age, it is also heavily taxed.

■ *Left:* Millesgården, the home, studio, and garden of Carl Milles, Sweden's famous modern sculptor, is also his final resting place. Though he lived abroad for long periods, eventually becoming an American citizen in 1945, he was extremely fond of his place on the island suburb of Lidingö. The beautifully terraced gardens overlooking an inlet of the Baltic provide a superb setting for replicas of Milles' best work, including this sculpture called, "Hand of God."

he cheapest hard liquor now sells for $25 per 750 milliliters. Nevertheless, the state has an important argument: one-third of all car accidents are related to alcohol, and excessive drinking leads to a variety of complications that demand medical treatment. Since these expenses are paid for by the state, it feels justified in levying taxes to pay for them, but these taxes still do not cover the medical costs caused by alcohol. Resolving such cause-and-effect problems is part of Sweden's dilemma.

Taxes are another issue Swedes discuss endlessly — one foreigners always hear about. The sales tax stands well over 20 percent now, but it is incorporated into the prices of items on the shelf, not added at the cash register. Income taxes are also high and progressive; the more you make, the more they take. One of the effects of these high taxes has been the growth of an "underground," or barter, economy, where services and goods are traded informally and not reported to the tax authorities. Some also claim high taxes reduce productivity by eliminating the incentive to work more in order to earn more. But the most important result has been tax fraud. The tax debate in Sweden usually deals with issues of solidarity and tax evasion, with the media often focusing on individuals who conduct business in Sweden but who have changed their residency and bank accounts to another European country. Tax returns are public information, and evening newspapers often publish the newly released tax returns of wealthy persons who have managed to pay no taxes.

Not only do the authorities scrutinize all tax returns, they also conduct investigations. There are famous cases of the excessive zeal with which the Swedish tax authorities have pursued the gathering of taxes. In 1976, film and theater director Ingmar Bergman was taken from a rehearsal by the police to answer questions about suspected tax evasion. Both his and his attorney's houses were searched by the police in pursuit of evidence. This affair generated a big debate about the power of the state bureaucracy to intrude into the private lives of citizens, especially since Ingmar Bergman eventually ended up getting money refunded to him instead of owing any taxes. Bergman received a public apology from Prime Minister Olof Palme but was so disgusted he temporarily moved abroad in protest.

■ *Right:* Valborg, on the eve of April 30, is a big occasion for traditional songs and feasting. While university students listen to songs and speeches hailing the end of the dark cold of winter and the return of the sun, evening parties all over Sweden are also singing in the spring, often around large community bonfires.

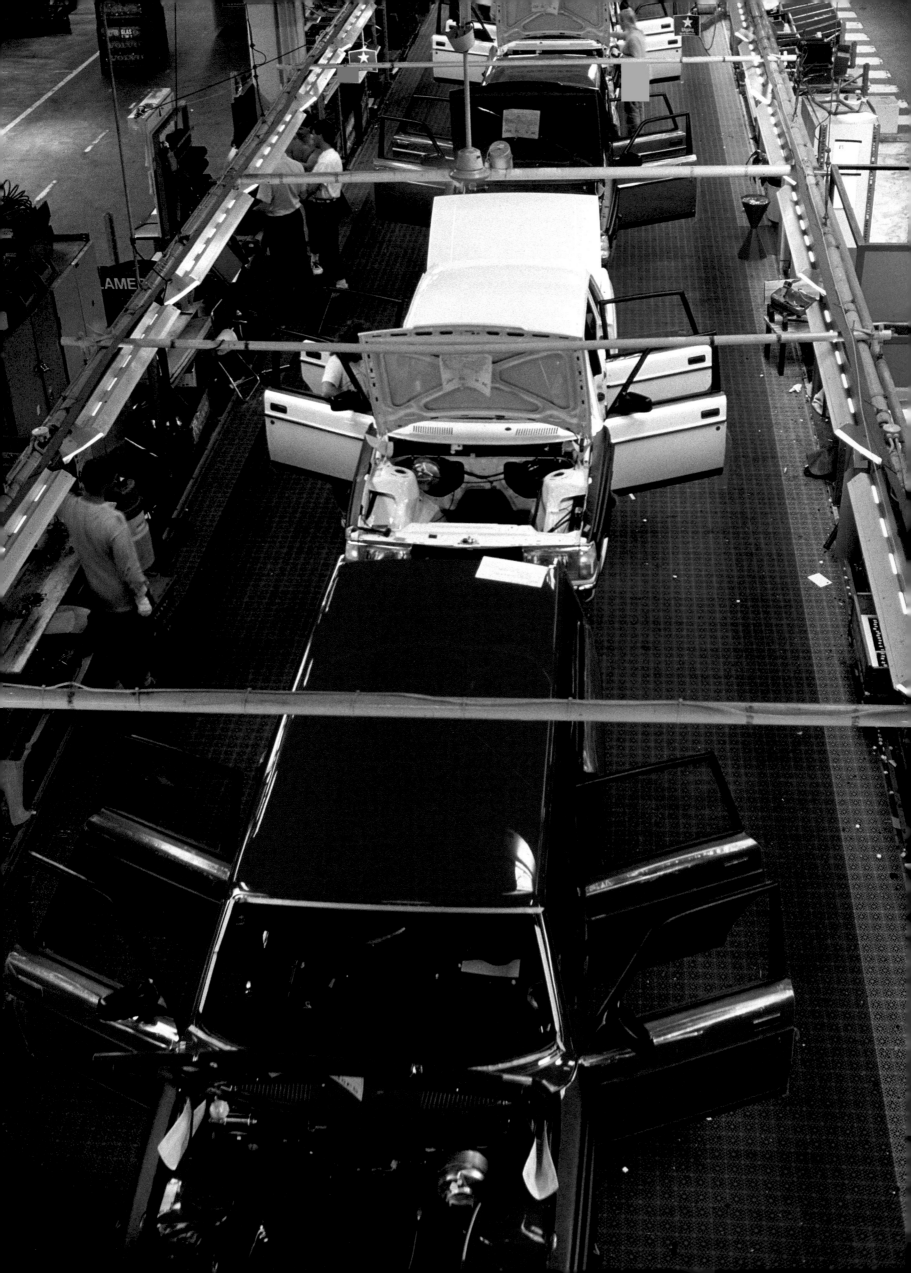

nother famous tax case involved author Astrid Lindgren, creator of the famous Pippi Longstocking character. In 1976, she was asked to pay 102 percent of her income for the previous year! Attitudes toward tax authorities did not improve when it was discovered, in 1983, that the Minister of the Judiciary, Ove Rainer, used tax loopholes and managed to pay virtually no tax at all on his huge income. The event was an ideological embarrassment for the Social Democrats, who have always argued that fair taxation is a demonstration of solidarity; the minister was forced to resign.

No country will ever become a utopia, not even Sweden. But Sweden has managed to bring about serious social progress and an evenly distributed sense of well-being. Hunger and abject poverty have been eliminated; every citizen is provided with decent housing, free education (including university studies), medical services available at a nominal amount, generous pensions, five weeks of paid vacation, and child support. About 20 percent of public spending is used for social and welfare services. Taxes are, without any doubt, very high, but Swedes and visitors alike are provided with an equally high level of state services. The political debate of what to finance and how to raise the money is, of course, eternal, one that is certainly not unfamiliar in the United States.

Americans seem to be fascinated with Swedish suicide rates. It goes back to a speech President Eisenhower made in 1960 in which he tried to discredit Sweden's welfare programs. In his speech, Eisenhower referred to a socialist country in the north where "suicide has gone up almost unbelievably." The implication was, of course, that in spite of all the good things Swedish society provided, many people just could not take it. But the truth of the matter is that suicide rates are about the same as in other industrialized countries, even if they are slightly higher than in the United States. And this slight difference might only exist, as one Swedish ethnographer pointed out, because Sweden has the world's most honest and accurate statistics about suicide.

In Sweden, the period following World War II has also been characterized by immigration. The majority of the immigrants are Finns, but there are also many from Eastern Europe, the Middle East, Asia, Mediterranean countries, and South America.

■ *Left:* Volvo is second behind Asea (ABB) in group sales and near the top in the number of people they employ. Their main products for export are Volvo cars, as well as marine engines, trucks, and tractors. Volvo is part of the growing metalworking industry which includes machinery, transport, and electronic equipment. Major companies include Volvo, Electrolux, Asea, and Saab-Scania. These metalworks are the backbone of the Swedish export industry.

**A**lthough many immigrants have come to Sweden bent on improving their financial situation, a number of political refugees, especially from South America, have arrived as well. Immigrants composed of both groups make up close to 10 percent of the total population. It is estimated that every eighth child growing up in Sweden today is of immigrant descent.

In a country like Sweden, which lacks the traditions of the "great melting pot" of the United States, this has created some racial and religious tensions. Many of the immigrant children experience a cultural clash when they try to reconcile the language, culture, and values of their home environment with those of Swedish society. Criminal activities by immigrants are disproportionately high, indicating the difficulty of adjusting to Swedish society.

But the immigrants have also rejuvenated Sweden. Many that come are well educated and contribute with their skills, as well as bringing new religious and secular values into Swedish society. And last, but not least, they have introduced a variety of wonderful foods to the Swedish diet. Today, it is easy to get a good kebab for lunch, then finish off with a cappucino and a baklava. Thirty years ago, even pizza was unknown in Swedish restaurants.

Sweden faces a number of challenges, some of which undoubtedly will change the country and its way of life. Since exports of industrial products are so vital to the economy, the energy question remains a central issue. Swedish industry and the Swedish standard of living are based on an abundance of available energy. Because Sweden lacks any domestic sources of oil, coal, or gas, it is totally dependent on foreign imports of fossil fuels. The oil crisis in the early 1970s gave emphasis to energy conservation, which, among other things, resulted in a very energy-conscious building industry. As a result, Swedish standards for residential housing have become a model for other cold regions in the world. Still, energy is expensive. The price of gasoline in Sweden has now reached one dollar per liter, or about four dollars per gallon.

For a number of reasons, fossil fuels are not an ideal energy alternative for the future. One serious problem is acid rain, the effects of which have been well known for at least a decade in Sweden.

■ *Right:* A small stream steps down a slope in the Rapadalen of Sarek National Park. From these moss-covered crevices on a mountainside, the first drops begin to seep and trickle. Here, where springs are born and the melting snow slides beneath rocks, rivers are also born. The waters of the sea which came by air to the land are now cutting their first channels on the icy and green slopes, emerging out of their crystal mountain solitude, starting their long journey home.

 oils rich in lime can neutralize the sulfuric acid that results from the burning of coal and oil, but the soils in western Sweden and Norrland are very low in lime and are unable to recover. An initial consequence of acid rain is increased toxicity in fresh-water fish and damage to forests. Eventually, all life in a watershed is killed, and the trees begin to die. On the west coast, thousands of lakes have literally been sterilized and are now devoid of life, and many thousands more are threatened. Attempts have been made to spread lime on winter ice, but the problem is of such vast magnitude that only a handful of lakes can be saved this way. A further complication is that much of the acid is carried by the winds that blow in from other countries, pointing to the necessity of international cooperation.

The two significant domestic sources of energy in Sweden today are hydroelectric and nuclear. Because of the many large rivers that drain into the Gulf of Bothnia, hydroelectric installations started early in the century, so today there are very few major free-flowing rivers left. Sweden has the largest uranium deposits in Europe, which makes the twelve operating nuclear power plants seem rational from that point of view. But the unresolved problem of where to store spent radioactive fuel, as well as the potential of a disastrous accident, led Sweden to a national referendum on this issue in 1980. It was decided that the nuclear power plants would begin to close down in 1995, and be completely out of operation by 2010. It is clear that Swedish energy costs will soon climb, some say by as much as 10 percent annually.

Another challenge is the world's growing international tendency. As many Western European countries move toward a common market envisioned as the United States of Europe—with one currency, one labor market, and eventually one military defense—Sweden still leans toward independence and neutrality. Culturally, it faces similar challenges. Some claim Sweden has already lost whatever distinct cultural value system it once had. They point to the enormous impact American culture has had on Swedish life. This spans everything from blue jeans and sweatshirts to American intellectual thought. Half of all films showing at movie theaters in any major city in Sweden may be American, and Swedish book clubs always offer a substantial number of recent American novels in translation.

■ *Left:* Standing near the line that separates Lappland and Västerbotten, the Mårdsele Falls, here a cataract of fire ignited by sunset, are part of the Vindel River's free-flowing beauty. Because of today's constantly increasing need for electrical energy, there are now very few major wild rivers left in all of Sweden.

hereas hamburgers were virtually unknown in Sweden thirty years ago, now McDonald's restaurants are found in many Swedish cities. Young people listen to rock and roll, and even country and western has become an important part of the Swedish music scene. Swedish television viewers know as much about J. R. Ewing as anyone in the United States, and they follow *Falcon Crest* today as they did *Bonanza, Ironside,* or *I Love Lucy* a few years ago.

On the streets, one sees a surprising number of gas-guzzling, perfectly restored American cars from the 1950s or the early 1960s. Obviously, with today's high gas prices, they represent something more than just transportation. During the late 1980s, nearly seventy-five thousand Swedes visited the United States annually, almost one percent of Sweden's population. There is no question about a Swedish fascination with things American.

How significant are all the American manifestations one encounters in Sweden today? In a global age like ours, is Western civilization in the process of becoming one large monoculture? Perhaps it is, at least in some respects. Increasing international travel brings more and more people from diverse backgrounds into contact with each other. An urban, Western way of life, with two parents commuting to work and the children in day-care, is probably as common in Stockholm as in Seattle.

Through internationalization, an increasing number of reference points are similar if not the same all over the world, and this is true of mundane, daily objects as well as values and ideologies. In shaping people's views of the world, the power of television is as strong in Sweden as in the United States. And the political reality of the world ahead seems international as well. Indeed, it will have to be if we are to solve the challenges facing us in the future.

At the same time, the old cultural distinctions cannot be discarded overnight. Any seemingly internationalized Swede, no matter how much at home in the world, will continue to retain something distinctly Swedish, too. His understanding of history and geography, the seasons—even holidays—as well as his language, will remain unique. Scratch him, and you will uncover areas of blue and yellow in a very familiar pattern.

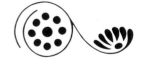

■ *Above:* When a high-altitude, many-colored, flashing luminosity, or aurora, is visible in the night skies of Sweden's polar zone, it is the northern lights putting on an eerie dance. An aurora occurring in the northern regions is called the *aurora borealis,* or northern lights, and in the southern regions, the *aurora australis,* or southern lights. Though not special to Sweden's Arctic area only, it occurs there in greater frequency and intensity. ■ *Below:* At minus 20° C near Stora Sjöfallet National Park, a beautiful full moon lingers on a clear day above the frozen Stora Lule River in this land of winter midday moons as well as summer midnight suns.

■ *Above:* Most peaks in the Scandinavian chain are over fifteen hundred meters (nearly five thousand feet) in height, with Kebnekaise the highest peak in Sweden at 2,111 meters (6,925 feet). ■ *Below:* In midsummer, the view looking up the Rapatjåkkå in Sarek toward the Äpar Range is illuminated by the light of the midnight sun. Though the sun usually drops behind the mountains in the fells, it still keeps the nights darkless, sending its rays down valleys to illuminate opposing slopes and high peaks. ■ *Right:* In 1910, Sweden was the first European country to establish national parks, mainly in the mountains of Lappland.

■ *Left:* Kukkesvagge River, one of the many rivers of Norrland with its origin tied to the glaciers and the precipitation-rich fells, flows along the border between Stora Sjöfallet and Sarek national parks. ■ *Above:* Sweden's inland waterways offer salmon, sea trout, trout, brown trout, char, pike, perch, and other species, all of which are available to the angler for small permit fees. ■ *Below:* The Voxna River runs through and helps drain Hälsingland Province. ■ *Overleaf:* Here near Ljungdalen in Härjedalen, a sunrise sends its golden light over a frost-covered marsh and the snow-capped Härjångs Mountains beyond.

■ *Left:* Twenty-five hundred of Sweden's fifteen thousand Saamis work with reindeer, now using snowmobiles, mountain bikes, and helicopters to round them up for separation, marking, and slaughter. ■ *Above:* Spread across four countries without a common language, Saamis struggle to maintain cultural identity. ■ *Below:* To commute to distant schools, Saami children are afforded unusual transportation—planes and even helicopters. ■ *Overleaf:* Half Sweden's land surface is covered with forest, most of it coniferous, like this pine forest in Medelpad. Wood pulp and paper products account for a quarter of all exports.

■ *Left:* Long-distance skiing used to be Sweden's most popular winter sport and still attracts large numbers of participants to races. However, Ingemar Stenmark's prowess on the alpine slopes boosted interest in downhill skiing. ■ *Above:* Even if summit ski lifts are not available on Åreskutan in winter, the cabin lift usually stays in operation for a panoramic view of the landscape around Åre. ■ *Below:* The wind-sculpted icescapes on Åreskutan demonstrate winter's cold artistic expressions, expressions that can remain year-round in Norrland, or become part of a river's passage to the east coast during spring melt.

■ *Above:* Lifts have been installed on new slopes everywhere, especially in places like Sälen in Dalarna and Åre in Jämtland. ■ *Below:* Not only is the land buried in winter, so are the waters in the Gulf of Bothnia along Sweden's east coast. Over this frozen prairie the sun barely shows itself from November to February, yet ice-breakers must keep the shipping lanes open between ports. ■ *Right:* Both country home and permanent residence illustrate the Swedes' love of wood and the abundance of timber for building. Spring or summer flowers, autumn leaves, or winter snow accentuate these simple, rustic designs.

■ *Left:* Nearly 15 percent of Sweden's surface is comprised of lakes and running water. ■ *Above:* When temperatures drop below minus 30° C, the celebration of nature is witnessed by few. Nature's architecture in winter carries a hard jurisdiction. ■ *Below:* Long-distance skating is the winter version of hiking, where boots are exchanged for ice skates. Here, skaters use the frozen surface of the Göta Canal to cross parts of Västergötland. ■ *Overleaf:* Sweden is one of the world's five leading ice hockey nations. The Globe is one of the symbolic structures of Stockholm and was host to the 1989 World Ice Hockey Championships.

■ *Left:* City Hall, *Stadshuset,* on Kungsholmen Island is topped by the golden national symbol, the Three Crowns, *Tre Kronor.* ■ *Above:* Water and sky, boats and islands are daily sights to visitors and residents of Stockholm. Here the ferry connects the island of Djurgården to the quay at the Old Town near Slussen. ■ *Below:* Stockholm, capital of Sweden and the "Venice of the North," is a city floating on water, connected by some forty bridges, and home for one-and-a-half million people. ■ *Overleaf:* Stockholm's past is neatly concentrated in the Old Town, *Gamla Stan,* which is known as the "city between the bridges."

■ *Above:* Yachting Day is the first weekend in September, when the waters of Stockholm become a dancing floor for over a thousand white sails. Participants come to compete on one of eleven courses in and around Stockholm. ■ *Below:* Djurgården is a perfect place for picnicking, jogging, walking, biking, horseback riding, paddling, boating, or sun bathing. ■ *Right:* Across from Skeppsholmen Island is Kungliga Slottet, the Royal Palace. Its construction kept the architects busy for forty-seven years. One of the world's largest palaces with royalty living within its six hundred rooms, Drottningholm today is home to the royal family.

■ *Left:* On this small island called *Gamla Stan,* "Old Town," Stockholm got its start more than seven hundred years ago. The cobbled lanes and winding alleys of the Old Town follow the original medieval street plan. Its old houses, places, and its soaring spires are steeped in history. ■ *Above:* Stockholm's Djurgården offers lovely pathways along a canal, giving an illusion of the countryside. ■ *Below:* The capital is situated on a number of islands where the fresh waters from Lake Mälaren flow into the salt waters of the Baltic. The link between these two waters is called *Strömmen.* The view is dominated by the Royal Palace.

■ *Above:* The dominant feature of the coastal town of Kalmar in Småland is Kalmar Castle. More a stronghold than a castle, within its Renaissance style is a system of bastions, ramparts, massive walls, and pointed spires. ■ *Below:* Just west of Stockholm on an island in Lake Mälaren is the royal family's residence, Drottningholm Palace, built from 1662 to 1681. The most enjoyable way to reach the palace is by ferry from near City Hall. ■ *Right:* The province of Skåne is densely populated, with excellent estates and some 240 castles. Vittskövle, near Kristianstad, appears to be a cross between a castle and a stately home.

■ *Left:* North of Gothenburg, the coast is frequented by sailors, bathers, and Atlantic storms. Waves from the North Sea have picked on the barren granite skerries since time immemorial, leaving them smooth and molded. Unlike the quieter Baltic waters, the restless North Sea never stops leaning on the land.
■ *Above:* The highest mountains and outer islands are primary holiday havens: one for the boot, the other for the boat. ■ *Below:* The Stockholm Archipelago starts in Stockholm, thus its name. The farther out one goes, the smaller the islands, the less the vegetation, and thus the greater the exposure to the elements.

■ *Above:* The Stockholm Archipelago offers myriad inlet passages for the sailing holidays of its million inhabitants. This narrow channel runs between Värmdö and Ingarö. ■ *Below:* This island off Dalarö is one of over twenty-four thousand in the Stockholm Archipelago. ■ *Right:* What could go better with quiet anchorage than a few potatoes, herring dishes, shrimp, and a cold beer or aquavit? ■ *Overleaf:* Högbonden Lighthouse, perched on a cliff above Ångermanland's wild coastline, combines its guardianship of the rocky shores with overnight accommodations as part of the extensive youth hostel association in Sweden.

■ *Left:* The Göta Canal is a picturesque system of canals, rivers, and lakes, affording navigable passage all the way across Sweden, from Stockholm to Gothenburg. ■ *Above:* Besides the thousands of pleasure craft that use the Göta Canal, old steamships also offer comfortable passage, with breaks for visits to historical castles and churches. ■ *Below:* Sweden is one of the richest lands in the world in terms of lakes, partly because it was mantled several times by ice. ■ *Overleaf:* The Åmål Church, with its old, carved wooden pews, pulpit, altar, and hymnboard, was constructed in the twelfth century in the town of Åmål.

■ *Left:* The island of Gotland, the largest in Sweden, offers idyllic nature, with lovely sylvan meadows, lime bogs, and alpine flora—relicts from the glacial period. ■ *Above:* The province of Gotland includes the islands of Karlsöarna, Fårö, and Gotska Sandön. Its capital, Visby, the "town of ruins and roses," is today a modern city, though much medieval architecture remains. Here at Almedalen Park in Visby are beautiful gardens and houses dating back to the thirteenth century. ■ *Below:* Of the over ninety medieval churches still in use on Gotland, the Visby Cathedral, St. Maria, is the sole one that remains intact.

■ *Above:* On the inland side of Öland, the waters are usually calmer and beaches are more common. Along the Kalmar Sound, on the northwest coast of the island at Sandvik is a lovely bathing area with crystal-clear water. ■ *Below:* Öland may be known as the island of windmills, but it is also the island of lighthouses. Keeping a watchful eye over the northern tip of Öland is *Långe Erik* "Long Eric" Lighthouse. ■ *Right:* At Öland's southern tip stands *Långe Jan* "Long John." Adjoining the lighthouse is a station of the Swedish Ornithological Society. So many birds migrate through Öland that telescopes outnumber tourist cameras.

■ *Left:* Högby Lighthouse stands watch on the northeast coast of the Baltic Sea.
■ *Above and Below:* The livelihood of this old fishing village was affected by two events connected to the United States. First, prohibition in the 1920s destroyed its mackerel exports since smoked fish was not in demand without alcohol. The second was World War I when the Germans laid mine fields in the North Sea, putting a stop to the mackerel fishing for which Gullholmen was the center.
■ *Overleaf:* The little island village of Hermanö connected to Gullholmen, is actually the oldest fishing village in Sweden, dating from the sixteenth century.

■ *Left:* Second-largest in population and home to Sweden's greatest shipyard, Gothenburg, or *Göteborg,* is the main entrance to Sweden. Here a passenger ship slips under the Älvsborg Bridge on its way into the thirteen-kilometer (eight-mile) long harbor. ■ *Above:* One-third of Sweden's imports and one-fourth of its exports pass through Gothenburg's harbor. Gothenburg's newest building, the Skanska, stands near Lilla Bommen, and the modern arch offers an interesting contrast to the old "Viking" four-masted barque. ■ *Below:* One of Gothenburg's main attractions is Liseberg, an amusement park of international standard.

■ *Above:* At the Uddeholms steel plant in Hagfors, raw materials are melted in an arc furnace. Now over 40 percent of all Swedes work in industry. ■ *Below:* Saab cars are manufactured by Saab-Scania, Sweden's fourth-largest company. Saab-Scania also produces jet fighters, guided missiles, and technical equipment and is involved in computer systems. ■ *Right:* Mining accounts for 1.4 percent of the market value of Sweden's industrial production and employs 1.2 percent of its industrial labor force. The LKAB mines are the world's largest underground iron ore mines, with four hundred kilometers (250 miles) of roads inside the earth.

■ *Left:* Lumps of molten glass are removed from special furnaces, then shaped into objects. The special melting pots, also made at Orrefors, insure the purest crystal possible. ■ *Above:* Småland is famed for its small industries that deal with leather, wood, and plastic, and — perhaps best known of all — glassworks. ■ *Overleaf:* Long associated with farming, especially in wooded areas, is the field fence known as *gärdsgård,* a hurdle-stake fence of wooden poles and split timber.

■ *Above, Below, and Right:* In carving a farm out of Småland terrain, trees were cut, rocks moved, and meadows and farms fenced with low stone walls, which tell the poverty of the soil and the energy of the farmers. According to legend, Saint Peter was to blame for this handicap. Having obtained permission to create this region, he made rather a mess of it. So God created the *Smålänning,* an enterprising "never-say-die" person, like Karl Karlsson here. Karl helped carve out his farm near Vrånghult and has survived there for seventy-eight years. He will happily continue do so until he gets to discuss the matter with Saint Peter.

■ *Left:* The Hälsinge-Hambo Folk Dance Festival comes on the first Saturday after the first Sunday in July in the province of Hälsingland. Twenty thousand visitors to Hårga, Bollnäs, Arbrå, and Järvsö watch more than three thousand participants compete in this event. ■ *Above:* On Midsummer, every community has a maypole, music, and dancing. In the province of Dalarna, fiddlers lead villagers and a wagon full of children down a country lane to the village green.

■ *Above:* All over Sweden, people celebrate Midsummer Eve, which comes on the weekend nearest June 24, with Midsummer Day on Saturday. Many folk traditions are associated with this festive event, the climax of the year, when the sun is at its highest point. Maypoles are raised in city parks, village greens, and private gardens such as this one at Skansen Park in Stockholm.

■ *Above:* On the morning of Midsummer Eve Swedes decorate their homes, cars, churches, and pavilions. In the afternoon they decorate the maypole, which comes from the Swedish word, *maja,* meaning "to make green." Leafy branches of birch are twined around the pole, and usually two circlets of flowers are hung from its crossbar, such as this one being attached in the village of Tibble in Dalarna, the province in which this public holiday is best known and attended.

■ *Above and Right:* Midsummer is the essence of celebration in Sweden, bringing out the best of both land and people. Children gather flowers and smiles from the fields; ladies weave garlands of leaves for the maypole and house, and flower wreaths for the head. Food, drink, folk music, dancing, and traditional costumes all blend together with the energy of the summer sun in delightful culmination.

■ *Left:* Lucia is celebrated on December 13 — according to tradition, the longest night of the year. Lucia morning is celebrated everywhere: in communities, homes, offices, schools, clubs, and some churches. ■ *Above:* On Lucia Day, children visit old-age homes to share traditional songs and food. ■ *Below:* Miss Lucia — dressed in white gown and a crown of candles — is accompanied by her white-clad attendants. They visit homes for senior citizens, hospitals, hotels, and Nobel Award winners. ■ *Overleaf:* Due to long years of peace, before 1983 there was no symbolic day of liberation. Now June 6 is celebrated as Flag Day.

■ *Above:* On Flag Day, the Royal Family visits Skansen, Stockholm's open-air museum. Traditional costumes are also donned all over Sweden on June 6.
■ *Below:* Swedes may celebrate the New Year by inviting in a few friends, and many greet the coming year in front of their television sets. The midnight fireworks show makes the skyline of Stockholm become one long colorful explosion. ■ *Right:* Flag Day is celebrated in schools and with parades, speeches, brass bands, and fireworks. Here the silhouette of the City Hall in Stockholm is dwarfed by explosions reflected across the waters of Riddarfjärden.

■ *Left:* The Nobel ceremony at the Concert Hall, attended by special invitation only, is followed by a banquet and dancing at the Town Hall. Food is served in the Blue Hall, which is actually red. Then the Golden Hall becomes a giant ballroom. ■ *Above and Below:* Nobel Day is celebrated on December 10. From a grant left by Alfred Nobel, who invented dynamite, the Nobel Foundation gives awards in physics, chemistry, medicine, literature, and peace. The ceremony in the Concert Hall in Stockholm is attended by King Carl XVI Gustav, Queen Silvia, and Princess Lilian. The king presents the awards to Nobel laureates.

■ *Above and Below:* In Sweden's winter darkness, Christmas means something more. Candles fill windows and rooms; warm *glögg* and fires warm heart and home; gingerbread houses are baked and decorated; skis, sleds, and sleighs stand outside northern homes with Christmas trees; and children are starry-eyed. ■ *Right:* It is interesting to compare a *Julbord,* or old Christmas table's fresh cheese, baked bread, beer, aquavit, and roast veal or lye-cured fish with a modern menu. Today the cheese, bread, and beer are still there, but the fish is stockfish and marinated herring, and the meat is more likely to be ham.

■ *Left:* Nowadays the whole of December is affected by the celebration of Christmas. By the time First Advent arrives, Christmas fairs have already begun and choirs are performing in churches such as here at Katarina in Stockholm. ■ *Above:* A long tradition vying for equal importance with the tree, food, and presents is watching Disney Cartoons on television at 3 P.M. The number of switched-on televisions for that one hour is equal to the number of switched-on Christmas trees. ■ *Below:* Christmas festivities involve traditional activities, which include the Christmas tree, the special meal, and the visit of Santa Claus.

■ *Above:* The Swedes' love of nature resulted in a right called *Allemansrätt,* or "every man's right." This gives everyone the right to walk or camp in woodlands and fields — even on private property — to pick flowers, berries, or mushrooms as long as the rights of owners are respected and nothing is damaged. ■ *Below and Right:* Apples, berries, mushrooms, leaves, or flowers are not just picked to fill cellars and freezers and vases; they also provide a source of exercise fashionable long before Swedes learned to jog or do aerobics. ■ *Overleaf:* Beech woods such as this in the province of Skåne once covered much of southern Sweden.

■ *Above, Below, and Right:* Summer is the season when Swedes start to drink in the sunshine, the season when their inborn love of nature draws families together in shared celebration. The *söndagsutflykt,* or the "Sunday outing," certainly can be any day of the week. Poetry and pictures seem to express it best, as Israel Kolmodin, the seventeenth-century poet, wrote in *A Summer Song:* "Now comes the time of flowers/ With beauty, joy and play, Now fields and woodland bowers/ Fresh, fragrant garbs display. All earth awakes to gladness/ As if by magic touch, Gone are the days of sadness,/ We did not mind them much."

■ *Left and Above:* Solar energy, or lack of it, has a lot to do with disposition in Sweden. The Swede endures long winters with little or no sunshine. From eighteen hours of darkness each day, to the endless days of summer, the "Swedish personality" fluctuates to the same extremes. When you make a friend with a Swede, it is often a friend for life. They are like the turtle in friendships, slow but steady. The disciplined Swede is over-organized, not quite trusting enough, but endearing and enduring in friendship. ■ *Below:* Heading out with the children, a basket, and a picnic lunch is a common pastime, keeping Swedes close to nature.

■ *Above and Below:* Spring in Sweden is poetically enchanting and is perhaps best portrayed both visually and in verse. Seventeenth-century poet Johan Runius wrote in *From Springtime*: "Sweet Spring is here, the fish begin to frisk about/ The tender blades of grass from their long sleep peep out,/ Wherever ear can hear, wherever eye can see/ All things for joy by leaps and bounds move smilingly." ■ *Right:* A survey in 1989 stated that Sweden had the best equal rights record for women of any country in the world, both in civil and social areas. Of course, there is always a little room for improvement, as seen here!

■ *Left:* Many families save for years to get a cottage in the country or along the coast. Some have inherited their little spot in the woods, while others try to make that cottage their permanent residence. Rather than a "get-away," many prefer to "stay away" from the urbanization that now is home to 80 percent of Sweden's population. ■ *Above:* A long-standing stereotype of Sweden is the beautiful blond; however, the face of Sweden includes ever-fewer blonds.

■ *Above:* One thing the Swede loves to make is music and song. Every celebration, season, and festival has its traditional songs. If an individual is not involved in physical sport, it is a safe bet that he or she is a member of a choir. Music comes in its regular daily doses, and then in extra servings during holidays and festivals.

■ *Above and Below:* The limitations of all language make music in Sweden especially important as music bridges all cultural barriers, whether it be a jazz group at Stampen in Stockholm's Old Town, Dixieland music on the square at Hötorget, a country singer at a fair in Värmland, rag tag students in Uppsala on Walpurgis Night, fiddlers playing folk tunes during midsummer celebrations in Dalarna, a choir at Katarina Church in Stockholm for First Advent, or a night at the Concert House with the Stockholm Philharmonic. Music and the social life it involves is nourishment for the soul and a vital part of Swedish life.

■ *Above:* This fully restored eighteenth-century theater, the Drottningholm Court Theater adjacent to the Royal Palace, is unique in that its thirty original sets, stage machinery, and props are in perfect working order and still in use. Except for lighting—electricity has replaced candlelight—nothing has changed since King Gustav III attended opera performances here. ■ *Below:* There are twenty-six publicly funded theaters in Sweden, including the Royal Opera and the Royal Dramatic Theater, both in Stockholm. Besides the Royal Opera in Stockholm, music theaters thrive in Gothenburg, Malmö, Karlstad, and Umeå.

■ *Above:* Ballet companies, such as the Stockholm Opera Ballet shown here, operate in association with the theaters in Gothenburg, Malmö, and Karlstad, as well as in Norrköping/Linköping. There are also about a hundred independent professional theater and dance groups in Sweden, most of them in major towns. In all, the institutional theaters and independent groups stage some twenty thousand performances annually, before a total audience of four million.

■ *Above:* Swedish sportsmen like Björn Borg, Stefan Edberg, and Mats Wilander in tennis, and Ingemar Stenmark in alpine skiing have ranked as world leaders. In tennis, Sweden has won the Davis Cup four of the last six years. The tennis capital and site for Davis Cup competition is the small west coast town of Båstad.

■ *Above and Below:* The Swedish sports movement is well-organized and takes good care of the young people coming up. The steady growth of interest in physical activity is reflected by the mass arrangements which are growing more popular every year. Two classic events are: The Lidingö Race is a thirty-kilometer (eighteen-mile) cross-country run around the island of Lidingö in autumn. The Vasa Race, *Vasaloppet,* the biggest cross-country ski race in the world is held in Dalarna on the first Sunday in March. This ninety-kilometer (fifty-five-mile) race between Sälen and Mora tries to limit itself to twelve thousand participants.

■ *Above:* The second Saturday in May is carnival time, or *Quarnevalen.* Invented by students at Stockholm's Technical University, it is a chance to compete with other university branches. ■ *Below:* Spring begins on April 30, the Feast of Valborg, or Walpurgis Night. The wildest celebrations are in university towns like Lund where students parade across the campus and through town, singing songs before dancing the night away and seeing spring's first dawn. ■ *Right:* On April 30, at exactly 3 P.M., in the old university town of Uppsala students put on their white students' caps and head down the hill from the University Library.

■ *Left and Above:* The Crayfish Premiere arrives on the second Wednesday in August. On that evening or some evening during the weeks following, friends gather on terraces and balconies under paper lanterns to feast on these little delicacies. Here people are prepared to pay almost any price for these tasty crustaceans. This yearly ritual, quite unique to Sweden, is when people crack open that first boiled crayfish of the year, combine it with bread and cheese, and wash it down with beer, wine, or perhaps aquavit — and a lot of singing. ■ *Below:* Another favorite delicacy is smoked herring, or *Böckling.*

■ *Above:* The northeast coast of Småland retains an alluring character, such as this inlet on Händelöp east of the Västervik. Here Karl-Erik Ericsson keeps his rowing arms in shape. ■ *Below:* Extending between Sweden's two largest lakes, Vänern and Vättern, is the province of Västergötland. This populated area was one of the first settled, and some have even claimed it is the true cradle of the Swedish state. ■ *Right:* Sweden is a water-rich land. Waterways have two main feeding periods in spring: May when the snows melt in the forests, and June when the snows from the glaciers and fells melt. Sweden's wet climate provides the rest.

■ *Left:* The Church of Sweden is admired more from without than within. This is the Stavnäs Church in Värmland. ■ *Above:* In summer, fields of yellow rape are common in southern Sweden. In one century, Sweden has evolved to where only 4 percent of its labor force is in agriculture, yet agriculture remains important to the economy. ■ *Below:* Thousands of Swedes have vacation homes in the country or on the islands. The typical little "red country cottage" is an undying characteristic of Sweden. ■ *Overleaf:* Such fields and seventeenth-century-style houses as these at Stensjö were frequently seen by those who settled in Småland.

■ *Left:* The early inhabitants of Bohuslän left many monuments and engraved figures. High on cliffs by the sea stand mighty grave cairns, while inland on flat slabs of rock are stone carvings. These carvings at Tanum were made during the later Bronze Age. ■ *Above:* At Kåseberga in Skåne is the Ales Stenar, fifty-eight large stones set in the shape of a boat sixty-seven meters long (220 feet). The outline of a Viking ship, the stones were set between 800 and 1050 A.D. ■ *Below:* The Baltic islands are too far south to catch the Midnight Sun, but summer sunsets are enough to soothe the soul of any Swede in love with his native land.

■ *Above:* On the afternoon of Midsummer Eve, fiddlers at Rättvik in Dalarna welcome the villagers who wear their regional costumes and carry the blue and yellow of Sweden. The festival, the most popular of all holidays in the country, begins in the morning and continues throughout the day and evening. Thousands of visitors arrive to observe these colorful festivities each year.